ASCENT/DESCENT

ASCENT/DESCENT

Walter Wangerin, Jr.

CASCADE *Books* · Eugene, Oregon

ASCENT/DESCENT

Cascade Books
An Imprint of Wipf and Stock Publishers
199 W. 8th Ave., Suite 3
Eugene, OR 97401

www.wipfandstock.com

PAPERBACK ISBN: 978-1-7252-8030-4
HARDCOVER ISBN: 978-1-7252-8029-8
EBOOK ISBN: 978-1-7252-8031-1

Cataloguing-in-Publication data:

Names: Wangerin, Walter, author.

Title: Ascent/descent / Walter Wangerin Jr.

Description: Eugene, OR: Cascade Books, 2020.

Identifiers: ISBN 978-1-7252-8030-4 (paperback). | ISBN 978-1-7252-8029-8 (hardcover). | ISBN 978-1-7252-8031-1 (ebook).

Subjects: LCSH: Poetry. | American literature—Poetry.

Classification: PS3573.A477.A61 2020 (print). | PS3573 (ebook).

Manufactured in the U.S.A.   AUGUST 20, 2020

For Scott Cairns

We turn and turn in the animal belly, in the mineral belly, in the belly of time.... To find a way out: the poem.

From Octavio Paz "Toward the poem."
Translated by Eliot Weinberger

Aeneas pressed through tangled underbrush
To gain the door to hell.

Scott Cairns, "Three Descents"

Contents

PART 2: *KINDER- UND HAUSMÄRCHEN*

PART 3: IN THE SPIRIT OF RILKE'S *BOOK OF HOURS*

PART 4: EIGHT DESCENTS

PART 5: FINIS

SYNTAX

Poets are the tractors that plow
undiscovered fields,
that furrow the fields
with linear verses.

The spiked teeth
of the poet's harrow
search for sense
and seek to speak.

The poet reaps
his fields,
binding the sheaves
with strings of syntax,

then builds bigger barns
wherein to store his grain.

PART 1

Virginia and Walter

Two strings, one pierced cry.

From Rita Dove's *Thomas and Beulah*

I. ST. LOUIS, MISSOURI

Virginia, 1941

"Don't get me started on those wash-eyed coppertops."
Walt and Virginia are sitting beside each other
on a stone bench in her father's the cemetery.
She's slicing Winesaps. Apples are promises.

"That befreckled exclamation point (don't get me
started), that water-eyed gingerman—
he rapped on the front door. A butterfly's kick.
I stared disdainfully down from my bedroom window.

Mother let him in. He kitten-mewed,
"Is your daughter here? *Gone with the Wind*'s at the Fox."

Let him take a streetcar, watching the torn curtains
that flap out the windows of passing tenements,

where women in nightgowns sit at the sills
combing and combing their desolated hair.

GOD AN' DE DEBIL IS COUNTIN' OUT THE DEADS, 1923

1.
During the prohibition Emil brewed
beer in his basement and sold it on the down-low.

Wilhelm would send his daughter up Bates, swinging
an empty beer-pot and singing, "To market, to market."

Her father's graveyard wall was to her left,
and across the street to her right Teutonic windows

flashed a glare and blameful sunlight at the girl.
"Flighty, that one. No respect for her elders."

Genia's dash was whippet-quick. Her hair
flew behind her like a sky of mares' tails.

A nickel bought a pot of beer. But Wilhelm
paid in kind, coming when Emil called.

2.
There came a day in August when the sun seared
St. Louis, and the air was so hot that the girl felt
the shadows of telephone wires crossing her skin.

Descending Emil's concrete steps to his basement,
Genia heard a devil's yell—
            a besotted
Karl, cursing in German, "*Gottes Verdammt!*"

His wiry body vibrated anger, his fists
were balled to take on all comers.
Emil hollered,
"Genia, get your papa!"

When Wilhelm came
he seized the back of Karl's belt and his collar,
carried the flailing drunkard to the graveyard, and tossed
him over the wall among the tombstones.

"Karl, Karl, *Gott und das Teufel* are counting:
who's gonna die from drink, and who ain't *gonna* die."

HOW IT HAPPENS, 1942

1.

Wilhelm whiskers schnapps. Walt lips foam—
two men meditating in a brown study.
Wilhelm says, "Take my keys, *Mann*. But *vorsicht!*
Watch out! My Ginia ain't no Fuller Brush."

Walt and Virg cross the Missouri in a pickup.
They spread a blanket beside Cahokia Downs.
Merlot and cheese, and Virg says, "What do you think?"
        "It's going to rain."
                  "No, Walt. What do you *think?*"

"About?"
        "About, do you love me?"
                Walt plucks up
a blade of crab grass and puts it between the hollows
of his thumbs and blows a quack. He corks
the Merlot, and stands, and says, "We have to go."

"*You* go." Virginia, as willful as the bitter
Naomi, forebodes a headstrong future. "I'm staying!"

2.

Next evening, while sitting on the stone bench,
the mute Virginia nibbles a soda cracker,

and the garrulous Walt crunches a sour pickle.
God, what a dazzling day! All's well in the world!

Walt winks. "My girl's a girl in a marble tower."
Virg doesn't answer that absurdity.

"Recriminate me not, Rapunzel, Rapunzel.
Let down your hair, and I'll climb it up to tup you"—

a randy tomcat to her a cat-o'-nine-tails.

Walt slips a slim, beribboned box from his pocket.
"As to your question, my Serenity—"

Virginia unribbons the box. Here on white satin
lies a moon-silvered locket etched with one word:
        "Yes!"

SECOND THOUGHTS

As I understand it a triumph's a wedding,
a charge to the rail, a retreat to the bedding.
But who will enlighten my father's first son
and tell me with sympathy which of us won?

2

Or think that engagement's a weary surrender,
the end of a prancing, magnificent bender.
I watch what Finalities will limit my sin,
and fear the hangover soon to set in.

3

Merciful God, won't you countenance wending?
Must all of your highways be straight and unbending?
A mouth to the south of me, which is my mother's,
and forth to the north of me—lo!—is another.
But God says, "Through much tribulation and sorrow
ye enter the kingdom." I marry tomorrow.

II. OREGON

The ascent, July 1943

1.

Cradled a Lutheran, coddled an incurable Lutheran,
Walt climbs the seminary's ladder to ordination.

Not schnapps, now. Kentucky bourbon straight,
and congenial stupors.

Walt buys a used, forbearing
'31 Chevy, then he and his wife strike out

across wind-swept fields of russet wheat,
and down mountains toward the rolling blue Pacific.

2.

In Vanport Walt pastors a small-town tinker-church.
Oh, that Reverend Dashing-Suiter-of-Souls!

Virginia's drill rewires the electrical circuits.
Her wrench plumbs pipes. Resolve sets her teeth.

Christ is Time. Walt is God's clock's sprocket,
and Virginia the engineer of passion and laughter.

PRELIMINARY BEDWORK

1.

Virginia, her hair caught back in a blue bandanna,
windexes the windows. She shakes Old Dutch
Cleanser into the bathtub and sponges it.

The Old Dutch box is a picture of a wroth, dwarfish
crone, her head hooded, her nose protruding,
her hand shaking a threatful and dangerous stick.

Virginia waxes her hardwood floors sock-slick,
while Roy and Dale are singing on a tinny
radio, "Happy trails to you, till we meet. . . ."

2.

Her gentleman caller comes through the front door,
his heart pumping chocolate covered cherries.
"Oh, come, my love, and go to bed with me."

His stick threatens nothing but felicity.
Her reception's slick is an avid anticipation.

+ + +

1.

Your smiling, vermillion lips. Your cerulean eyes.
Your breasts mounds of lilies. Your thighs inviting.
Your slender arms urbane. Your hips wingéd.
Your fawn-feet frolicking on green hills.

2.
Your father's hair is snow on the holy mountain,
and yours is a black cascade down the face of that mountain.

3.
Those satin lips! Those fetching sapphire eyes.
Your breastmilk rich and explicitly delicious.
Your arms Pietas. Your feet the feet of a ewe.
Your tread lightsome as you graze in green pastures.

4.
Your father is Moses in a papyrus basket,
and you are the sister that watches over him,

5.
and I am King David, piping my sheep to me,
David, who knows the names of his every lamb.

CIRCUS

I march to trumpets and endorse the idiot
confusion of snare drums when I perform.
Trombones are the tide behind, and women giddy at
my slashed, howling red uniform.

I ride elephants, scorn tigers, embrace
apes and trust that heaven is no higher
than a particular, pluperfect wire.
And when I breathe, enormous tents take place.

The towns I enter shake sleep from their eyes.
They peer out their windows. Well, should they cheer?
The children do. Stores go blank. Old men
and young women start laughing past surprise.

The jingle-ringing towns say, "Yes!" A cock-eyed, striped parade
they, "Yes!" have room for.
　　　　Virginia! You are the village I invade.

REVEREND VERSIFIER

This poem is to woo you
to the close consideration of two
eggs.

Marry one to Oscar Mayer
in a fryer—
this for dinner.

Allow the other the leisure
to con-descend to the ascending pleasure
of a sinner.

Your husband begs
two eggs,
one for dinner,
one for ardor.

Not in that order.

PARTURITION, FEBRUARY 13, 1944

The ukase of a red, elliptic scream
her forehead mortified, squirming with worms of pain.

Virginia's belly's primordial. God shouts
a firmament to dam back the wild waters.

Ahhh, her spirit floats from this bloodless room,
she a dream ascending the empyrean.

The cosmos embraces her. The spheres sing
an unheard music: *Lullay, lullay, myn lyking,*

Suddenly Virg is back under fluorescens,
cursing her vulvar, bleeding delivery,

cursing the legacy of mother Eve,
and the pastor who's not here to comfort her.

No, he's preaching a correlative sermon: "Plow
the earth, Lord, and plant your own conceiving seed."

THIS EXISTENCE

It's not the labor.
It's a choice.

That absurdly dense
rock in your woman-
womb—bear it!

More than six—
there will be others.

Choose dignity.
Turn purposelessness
purposeful. Choose *that*.

Abide the bloods
of childbirth.

Make the absurd
sensible.

III. SHELTON, WASHINGTON

Her second birth: June 25, 1945

Her hands steeped in a hot, slanderous dishwater,
Virg gazes out at Mt. Olympus—that rock

solid in the turbulence of souls;
that Attic footstool of immortality.

Walt serves a trifling church—an energetic
pastor, charming the people with baritone sermons.

Before communion he scratches Palmolive under
his nails so no one smells the reek of his Camels.

Virginia has delivered one child.
A second bucks like a warhorse in her womb.

Last winter the laundry froze stiff on the clothesline.
She stacked it inside and warmed it with lambent sighs.

Years hence Mt. St. Helen will blast off half
her head, spouting lava and a global smoke.

IV. CHICAGO, ILLINOIS

Stranded, May 1945

1.
Walt drives his family east. The ambitious
young pastor is congratulating himself
for ascending to the cirrocumulus summits
of the Church's hierarchy. He will direct
its international youth group. He'll ride the rails
to the states, speaking and playing a sly piano.

Wally leans on the back of his mother's
car seat, fond of her widow's peak.

She says, "Poppycock!" and the tip of her nose
nips down like the tip of a boy's cane pole,
then up when the flashing sunfish throws its bait.

Wally sniffs her hair. "You smell like a sandy beach."
"Oh, my little man! One day you'll be
a poet of sweet possibilities."

2.
The Martins purchase a house on Overhill Street.
Walt sells the Chevy and buys a baby grand
piano and moves into the living room.

Straightway he sits on its stool and strikes a chord
then makes a sour face. "It's out of tune."
With a tiny wrench he tunes the strings by ear,
then sits, gives his wife a wink, and plays,

"Oh, I lost my true lover, a-courtin' too slow."

Virginia says, "How will I get to the Red Owl now?"

Walt grins. "You pays your dime, you rides the bus."

But the bus is an iron womb, griped by a third
sufferance, and Virg is a child-tormented Rebekah
in whose cavern two stones fractured one another.

"Christ! Will my toilings *never* cease?"

HIS PLEA

The sunset is a brass tension when daylight
and darkness clash their antlers in the clouds.

Let sundown incarnadine the sky. Let it
turn the clouds into crimson featherbeds.

Twilight enwreathes the day. Birds nestle
on their broods. The cicada grinds his song.

The stars are the pinking shears that have snipped black
velvet. The moon's horns cradle hope.

Anger lags. The diurnal night swells
with well-being. The universe inflates.

The doe and her fawn lie down under apple trees.
If all of these, why not we? Oh, I pray

that the mild, conciliating night will ease
this tension between us, and we may go to bed.

THE EGOTIST, 1946

Walt buys a meerschaum then takes his wife for a walk,
beguiling her with smoke rings till the criminal wind
highjacks his vacuous O's.

       After supper,
and after putting her boys to bed, Virginia
drops exhausted onto the living room sofa.

Walt soothes her by playing a rain-soft Pachelbel prelude,
the Bach *Toccata and Fugue* in e-flat major.

Now Walt's the criminal: riffs on the Duke's, *It don't*
mean a thing if it ain't got that swing. Then, *Gon' get racy*
with Count Basie! Then, *Dig that jive to come alive!*

The man's self-indulgence shocks his wife awake,
sitting up and blinking in the dead-dark room,
lost in a hall of crashing blasphemies.

GRAVE DELIVERIES

The withered old woman,
that bitter old woman
Naomi entombed
her sons in her womb
as if their birthing
would be her dying.

Rachel *did* die
delivering
her son, Benoni.

Rebekah suffered
twins in her gut.

Parturitions
render a baby-shot mother
acrimonious.

THE CRONE, FEBRUARY 1947

Before their mother lies down and labors to bear
her third child, Wally and Paul are sent
to St. Louis and into their grandmother's Lysol house.

Ida's that Old Dutch dwarf, her tongue the hickory stick,
her shoulders hunch-backed with disappointment.

A *wop* of mashed potatoes, a slap of beets
boiled floppy. Sour cabbage. Inedible food.

Four-year-old Wally is Magdalene weeping tears
on the tomb, *his* tears falling on his stoneware plate.

Ida won't speak his name. She calls him, "*Ein Schwein.*
"Eat them beets, boy, like hogs swill slops."

The boy doesn't chew. He sucks the beets till nine
o'clock when misery has blacked the windows,
then spits them out as white as communion wafers.

PHILIP, MARCH 10, 1947

She thinks he says, "Appease the God in me."
He doesn't. He's frowning down between her thighs.

The doctor's facemask conceals his identity,
and his latex gloves his hands, and his greens himself.

She swears he says, "Appease the God in me,"
hisses and grabs her knees and leans gut-forward,

laboring to bear her lump of hurt.
Take care my God, my God! This hurt is my heart!

Her labor feels like the medieval rack
that stretched a captive's spine until it cracked.

Episiotomy. He lays the numb edge
of his scalpel to her extremest womanhood.

Blood rivers her buttocks. Her thighs drain dead grey.
I will never beseech a god who hides his face!

THE DISPOSSESSED

1.

Virginia presses the breastflesh below her infant's
nose so he can breathe while she suckles him.

Though her exposed intimacy is blameless,
Walt broods moodily over this mother and child.

Her hair is a dark water that breaks at the ear
and spills on the innocent forehead of her child.

To Walt the baby's tongue is utilitarian.
a rubber suction on his wife's privacy.

Little truckdriver, that's not a dashboard knob!
Virginia coos pigeon-sounds in her throat.

The boy smacks. Sweat beads his brow.
He swallows and sighs, sighs and swallows again,

2.

while Walt pockets his hands and retreats to the living
room—an alien in his own house.

V. GRAND FORKS, NORTH DAKOTA

Preponderance, Autumn 1951

1
The parsonage looks down a bluff to the Red River.

At flood the river's swift current bears uprooted
trees and dead hogs rolling over like barrels.

   Frightful!

2
        Here's Max yelling up to Wally's
window,
"Hey! Let's go down and sail my boat on the river!"
His hair's Scot-red and his freckles a zodiac.

Wally's cough keeps him home. Max sings, "The sailor's
off to the sea!" He goes down, and never returns.

3
Flashlights are torches searching the midnight shore.
Fathers supplicate upstream.

      Wally
envisions his friend's red hair undulating
like seaweed in green water, fish darting through it.

Oh, those sightless eyes. Oh, those freckles.

GARGOYLES

1.

Melancholia sits heavy on the boy's chest.
Random whips his sodden mouth. Claws scrape
his brainpan as barren as an abandoned village.
His apprehensions are fire-forged knives.

Thus: four ways of dying, and a fifth for death.

Weep, child. You have the right. Soak your sheets,
for no one sits vigil by you. Four candles burned
at the corners of your bed, but their wicks flamed out.
The smoke coils up and fingerprints the ceiling.

The child cries like a cub whose leg's been snapped
in the rat-snake's teeth of a hunter's trap.

2.

His door opens a crack. A vertical strip
of light. Wider, and there stands his mother,
a diaphanous, angelic silhouette.

HER SIXTH CHILD, NOVEMBER 17, 1952

1.
Her water breaks, saturating the sofa.
Contractions bind her belly like the leather straps
of farm machinery. Her cry startles her son.

Walt's busy about some sort of ministry.

2.
Virginia phones for a taxi, then rounds on the nine-
year-old Wally and growls, "Find your father!
Burn his ass! Get him to the hospital!"

God help him with Jeremiah's impossible task.
Where can he run? He has to care for his siblings.

Three a.m. Walt bursts in exploding snow.
"Wally, not in bed?"

            "Daddy! Where *were* you?"

"Walking Schmidt around his barn. Finding his stash,
and pouring his whiskey bottles out on the snow.
Go to bed. I'll go and sleep by your mother."

"She isn't here."

      "Where?

            "Having a baby."

The hanging judge hammers her courtroom to order.
She sentences the accused to a potter's field.
A man can die on the point of an angry eye

DESCENT # 1

Sheep graze safely in the church's dark nave. The organist is
resurrecting Johann Sebastian Bach.

It's Saturday night. Walt's written his sermon longhand—
a fountain pen and black ink and bold strokes,
all consistent with his character.

Mr. Rutell, who owned a haberdashery,
walked into the Red River. His spirit bubbled
on the water.
        Sheep grazed the green shore.

Walt plays "This World of Pain and Care," spreading
a hymnic turf on Mr. Rutell's absence.

A hymn of dolor let us sing, let us sing,
rooks and nightingales in harmony.

Mrs. Rutell's song is a howl in the pit
of her kitchen. "How long, O Lord? O God, how long?"

HER SPEAKING SILENCES

She says he talks like a jay.
Like a preacher with logorrhea.
Like a poet without portfolio.

She says this, standing at the stove
with ineffable eyes,
her tears spitting
in the pan of hot grease.

Says this with an unforthcoming countenance,
with plates set down with unspoken accusations,
with meals of mute reproach.

The preacher can exegete his wife's eyes.
Jeremiads. When the King comes riding his horse of glory,
he will cast the goats gnashing their teeth in a stygian darkness.

Then what should he do? Fall silent, too? And be eaten
by the parasitic words he does not say?

A TERMINATION

The wingless Erinys descends into Hades,
her homing hole, and threatens the dead who try
to rise. This boy rises from his own hell.

His mother is pushing a grocery cart up a Red
Owl aisle, six children goslings behind her.

Then Wally spies a rack of comics: Disney!
He sits on the floor and loses himself in the story—
out of clock-time into the timeless time of tales.

Exchanging Disney for Little Lula, he glances
up, *leaps* up. "Mommy!" The boy's been abandoned!
"*Mommeee!*"
            Virginia hears and wheels into sight.

"Come here, boy! Do *not* cover your face with your hands!"
She slaps his ear. He's too stunned to cry. *This,*
he realizes, *this is the end of endings.*

MOTHER OF THE EVENING

1

Love paints Virginia's nails a Saint's-day red.
Her crimson lipstick wreaths benedictions.

She glides into Wally's bedroom, her scent Channel
5. A red, auroral stripe descends
her black dress from the shoulder to the hem.

She sits down on the side of his bed, her weight
creating a scallop down which he rolls to her thigh,
that foundation firm with an abiding affection.

"Wally, Dad and I are off to the Himmels'—
bridge. Coffee for me. Gin for your father."

Virginia leans down and kisses her son's forehead.
"Angels' wings enfold thee, and the stars behold thee."

2

Love is visible. When Wally's parents are gone,
he looks in a mirror—and, oh, that smackaroo!

DOLLS CAN DIE

Gertrude Trask is Raggedy Ann on her bedsheet,
her face vacant for the loss of her button eyes,
stuffed with the batting of an incurable cancer.

Rev. Martin unlatches a box shaped like a small
black casket. He removes a small cruse of wine
and a wafer—elements of the Eucharist.

The pastor dips his forefinger in the wine,
brings a drop to a fragment of wafer, then touches
this tiny meal to Gertrude's torpid tongue.

Now there shall be no more anguish for her
that was caught in the black shaft of Death's throat.

The pastor replaces the blood and the corpse into
his casket. Death is a marionette hanging
from the finger-strings of an indifferent god.

MOTHER OF THE MORNING

There be *Harpies* here—female faces, hawks'
bodies, talons to rip small creatures bloody.

And there be *Ire* in this kitchen. Ire puts a match
to a burner and ignites a ring of blue buds.

She stands in crushed-backed slippers and a bathrobe,
her arm akimbo, her fist propped on her hip.

She's stirring a pot of oatmeal, her children passive.

Wally floats into the kitchen on a dawn-cloud
of kisses, his forehead still marked with the baptismal
benediction of priestly Mother Evening.

"Late!"
        Mother Morning scoops a spoonful of sodden
oatmeal and hurls the whole at her son. *"Remorse,* boy!"

Wally's chin begins to tremble. His mother
glares. You will walk! In slops! To school!"

DEATH AND HELL

The first line that Sir Patrick read,
A loud lauch lauchéd he;
The next line that Sir Patrick read,
A tear blinded his ee.

"O wha is this has done this deed,
This ill deed done to me,
To send me out this time o' the year
To sail upon the sea?"'

A small craft can be tossed up like a wooden chip on the ridge of a heaving ocean breaker, then pitched down into a trench of black water.

Jonah, in order to escape the Lord's command to preach in Nineveh, Jonah embarked on a boat plying away and away. A tempestuous headwind nearly founders the boat. The terrified captain questions his crew. They cast lots. The bones signify Jonah. He's thrown overboard and is swallowed by ineluctable judgment.

Paul, the prisoner of a Roman guard, boards a vessel bound for Rome. Time is a tyrant. By October the shipping lanes of the Mediterranean's violent waters are closed. But Rome will not be denied, so the ship's captain puts out to sea. Not two hours into the voyage a thunderstorm strikes the sea. Breakers lash the gunwales. Waves boil over the deck. Before the ship swamps, sailors climb the ratlines to reef the sails. But the boat heels so far to port that they drop like cloaked bats, bundles of misfortune. Sailors lower the lifeboats. The soldiers, the Roman guards, and all the passengers cram forward, preparing to jump into the boats to save themselves. Paul shouts, "It's a savage sea! Wait and see what my God will do!" "His God? *Our* gods!" The ship's prow shatters like a shell against a reef. What God can do! Every soul survives.

May 1915: Mary McFee has had enough of New York City. She and her daughter—also a Mary—occupy a cabin on the British liner *Lusitania* sailing for Liverpool. She's one among two thousand civilians. The seas have been calm, and the wind steady. No need to beseech the Almighty for safe passage and in Liverpool alive. But a German U-boat torpedoes the *Lusitania*. No one lives. All sink into watery graves.

Alive on the sea. Under its waters, dead. Birth and death bracket every life.

It was the king who wrote that letter to Sir Patrick, wrote it while dizzy in his cups. He's taken it into his head to enjoy a junket on his sailing ship. His letter arrives while Sir Patrick is walking the sandy shore.

Presently the king's ship is moored thirty miles from Dumferline town.

No poet, this king. Pedestrian in all his ways. The words he's given to speak are not his, but those of the balladeer who fashions the words:

> "'O where will I get a guid sailor
> To sail this ship of mine?'
>
> 'Sir, 'tis Patrick the best sailor
> That ever sailed the sea.'"

It's a weatherly dawn. The sea's heavings are the salt-bitter breasts of that screaming, primal goddess, Tiamat.

But a king's command will hang a disobedient man.

Captain Patrick Spens is about to weigh anchor when his pilot comes and warns him, saying, "Och, 'tis them black, belly-swelling clouds as rives me heart. And 'twas a dreadful omen that I saw.

Late, late yestre'en methought I saw
The new moon wi' the auld moon in her arm.
I fear, I fear, my dear Master
That we shall come to harm."

This boy's antagonizing mother is his rolling, retributory sea. He has learned—he has *had* to learn—to decipher her interior weather before she reads the signs herself.

In his book *On Christian Doctrine* St. Augustine wrote that a human's mood can be interpreted by her facial expressions, her physical behavior, the tones of her speech.

Paul Strand photographed a blind woman sitting in front of a cinderblock wall, the lids of her right eye occluding that eye's sight, while her left eye gazes at some drear thing beyond the photo's border. Strand reveals the depths of her hopeless, age-old weariness by these signs alone.

Rembrandt painted the prophet Jeremiah in dismal tones, a Bible open on his lap, his own eyes heavy because Judah has ignored the Lord God's warning that this stubborn people will be destroyed. Read dejection, and understand his heart.

If, before she enters the kitchen, the boy hears a hard tread; and if, when she enters, her face is a swart scowl and her lips the thin rinds of lemons; and if, when she speaks, her voice sounds like gravel crunched under a car's tires—then the portents are menacing.

But if the woman, wearing nothing but a bra above her midriff and a girdle below her midriff; and if she places her left hand on the kitchen counter and commences high-kicking her right leg to the rhythm of her gay lyric, "Praise the Lord and pass the ammunition, and we'll all be free!"—then the signs betoken a merriment, and the boy can laugh a loud laugh.

Aye, but it's sad to say that the first mother dominates.
And what began with the king's glad idea, ends unhappily.

"O lang, lang may ladies sit
Wi' their fans flippin' in their hands
Or e'er they see Sir Patrick Spens
Come sailing to the land.

Half o're, half o're to Aberdour
'Tis fifty fadom deep,
And under the brine lies guid Sir Patrick
Wi' the Scots lords at his feet."

+ + +

Father Zossima sits on a stool in his monastery's chapter-house. "Fathers and teachers," he says, "what is hell? I answer according the discernments of St. Isaac the Syrian. Hell is the torment of being unable to love.

"Once, but only once, in unending time and in limitless space, the spirit of an earthly woman was given the ability to say, 'I am, and I love.' Ah, but 'twas only the wink of a moment given to her to say that eternal saying. But she rejected love and did not love.

"After she departed the earth, the woman was that rich man who looked across a great gulf and saw Lazarus lying on Abraham's bosom."

Father Zossima pauses. He strokes his grizzled beard, and then continues.

"Here she was, divided by a minimal degree from the realm of Christ. 'Twas the nearness itself that tormented her with the andirons of hell. Here, finally, she loved with a Christ-like love, and yearned to enter heaven where she might love and be loved, but could not because she had refused to love on earth.

"Fathers and teachers, love is life. Love sacrifices itself. Love gives its life away for the sake of others. But this woman's eternity was her hell, for she had no life to sacrifice."

Because the boy's mother does not love him now, she will hereafter suffer the agony of loving and being unloved forever and forever.

GOD'S QUILL: FEBRUARY 26, 1954

Nature is the cursive of the Creator.
The diurnal days are not ashamed of their names.
Gender scrawls, "Together." Gender scowls, "Apart."
The leaves of the aspens whisper hymns on the wind.

The Creator's calligraphic symmetry is
the feeble hare that dens in the rocks of God;
the fish are a flourished script on the face of the waters;
the mothering fish protecting her children in her mouth.

After the shepherd has gnashed his shearing clippers
and sheared the ewe's lambs, she weaves wool
to cloak her children.
        The she-bear licks her formless
pulps into shape, and inscribes their names on their souls.

Virginia, your seventh child will not know herself
until you whisper her name and grant her being.

A BIDDING PRAYER

She sits at her window under moonlight, sewing
and praying, "Mother me that I might mother my own."
Snow pillows the sill of an ebony window frame.

The needle pricks the young queen's finger. Three drops
of blood print the snow with a triangular hope:

"Lips coral red, hair a midnight weft,
skin the complexion of sister moon at her full."

The world turns. The queen gives birth to her prayer,
then dies at "Amen."
           A king must have a queen. This king
weds a shrew who comes to loathe Snow White.

Wally lives this mystery, then comes to know
its meaning. He has *two* mothers—the Morning She,
jealous of the Evening She whose grace
is reflected in the gracious face of the boy.

VI: EDMONTON, CANADA, SEPTEMBER 1954

Petals red, petals blue

This garden grows roses and violets.
Pink rivulets irrigate their roots.

The garden is cloven into two hills
where red deer prance and foxes switch their tails.

The boy's mother commands him to measure his bushels
of blossoms in the bathroom mirror. "You *deserved* this!"

She sowed the seeds that will in autumn sprout the crimson
leaves that sycamores bleed on white snow.

Her boy has, by *God!* broken the stones
of Moses, commandments cracked by lightning bolts.

The Salt-Sea rod that enforced her fury is the handle
of the mop that beat the boy's impertinence.

Virginia's the gardener. Wally's the garden
that she trowels with a trowel's sharply-whetted edge.

RABID, SUMMER 1956

Psychologists will name the syndrome "dyslexia."
But the undiagnosed can't be diagnosed.
Virg will be damned if she can't teach her son
to read. This rank Psalmist opens her book.
"Read this." Michael tries, but reverses the phrases.

"For God's sake, these two words!" Michael reads
the first word right. The second word is whimpered.

"Shepherd!" Virg barks, her fingernail jabbing the word,
Shepherd. She slaps the Psalter with the flat of her hand.

Michael is Elijah, sustained by the food of angels.
But she who whacks him to the floor is chthonic.

My brother curls inward and weeps icicles.
Mother hisses, "Jesus Christ!" and stalks off.

Michael will not survive beyond the night
of CO in his parents' enclosed garage.

COLD COMFORT

"Those leaves," Walt says, "blown down from an autumn tree become the soil that feeds the spring-greening tree."

She says, "Dead is just dead. Accidents kill."

"Yes. Dead. But alive."

"In memory? Shit."

"No, Virg. Climb Olympus. Look down and see
time inside itself, and the flower in its seed.
One tree's a forest. One ring a hemisphere.
Our son's in the bud. He is the uncurling leaf—"

"Christ! What is not can never be again!"

"Ah, let me be the leaf and you the soil."

"Right! My vagina's supposed to be your bud?
And my pollen's supposed to beget you *more* children?"

"No. No, forget my foolish analogy.
Your son's dead. Our son is most certainly dead."

TRANQUILITY

Walt shovels a circle of snow in his backyard,
then hoses the bare earth to a sheen ice blue.

Walt's an athlete at hockey. He's bought ice skates
for his sons. Then he and Paul are whacking pucks.

Wally's ankles warp. He steps from the Sacred
Circle then stands—a cripple in the snow.

Evening deepens. Walt, son Paul,
and their swift motions recede into silhouettes.

The weary sun sinks. The winter sky becomes
a luminous, transcendent mother-of-pearl,

a soft empyrean, an exhalation of dreams.
The horizon is pricked by the shadow-points of pines,

and the sky's a vault so tranquil that a boy can sleep
on it, slipping from life into cold eternity.

DESCENT # 2, ALBERTA'S
CRUDE-OIL REFINERY

Across the North Saskatchewan River Valley
Gog's refining eyes fire the night,

each flame a diabolical torch in the hands
of savagery, bone-pyres for the ineloquent dead.

To save his siblings, Wally sits by their beds
and spins stories on his inventive distaff.

"Those torches on castle battlements guard us
by blinding the eyes of dragons and the sorceress."

His siblings sleep. He watches, fearing that Inferno
will to cross the valley with a murderous eye.

Wally's a savior without salvation. An unbodied
cross. A deviant. An unshriven priest.

There are no castles. No guardians. Only
this unsanctified boy and an unrepentant God.

AN EVIL WIND

After Walt was elected president of a small
college, and after affixing a sign to that effect
on his office door, he ran dead-straight into
the spit-fire sting of Dr. Neid's resentment.
"The presidency was mine!"

        His wife's
kitchen smells of cloves and cinnamon. "Avoid
Martin's mongrel son!"

        One boy says, "Snail,
come out your hole or I'll beat you black as coal."

The other says, "Snail, put out your horns,
and I'll give you bread and barely corns."

        The campus
air is sweet in Nied's nose. The foul-fogged
campus is a treacly bile in Walter's throat.

THE UNHOUSED DOVE

He lies prone on the floor, his head propped
on his palm, reading *Look Homeward, Angel*,
a novel that tells the tale of his family's crises.

Mr. Gant carves angels. Mrs. Gant
earns money renting out rooms in her boarding house.
Hawks build their nests with sticks on high crags.

Hate has no home. Gnashing teeth no house.

Wally's parents come mounting the stairs, Walt in front,
Virginia an antipathy behind.
"Die, Walt! Just die! We'd all be better off."
"You don't mean it, Virg. You don't mean it."

Their house is built of sticks and bitterness.
Their boy perches outside their quarrels, a dove
mourning the fall of his parents' habitation.

THE INFINITE AND THE FINITE

God sleeps. When his limitless hand drops on the earth
it batters humanity's limited ambitions.

You want to write poems? You'll never be a poet.
You hope for advancement? You will stultify.

Do you seek fame? Live in infamy.
Expect no portion to be apportioned you,

for you in the night are a nothing in a nowhere.
Walk the cosmos, sole and solitary.

I can't help you. The lonely can't companion
the lonely. God slumbers. If he wakes,

his cosmos will be a shroud starless darkness,
and his abyss a black pit for the 666.

In hades, where Charon plies the River Styx,
Erinys will menace us with her three-headed dog.

DESCENT # 3

The man's spirit is like the wax the candleflame
melts till it runs like tears down to its sconce.

His strength is annealing, his hopes receding—
no longer a citizen in his wife's domain.

He's leashed. Fenced. His evacuations have killed
the backyard grass. His Kibble's moss-moist. Say to him,
"Dry bones, you will never be fleshed again."

His wife rules with the club of that Dutch Cleanser
dwarf.
        He lives in the shadows of memory.

There was a time, ah, a time when he ministered
with a generous hand and a kindly authority.
But her saying is true: "What was will never be."

He clings to a wisp of religion. He survives on faith
and gin. Even a dog whimpers to live.

DESCENT # 4: LUNACY

Wally's shrill whistling condemns his deviant mother
who stalks her children, a great Goliath taunting them.

Wally's Perseus in his bedroom, his mother a howling
Medusa, turning unities into stone.

Wally would crack that stone to free his family.
But where's the hammer that can shatter granite?

Cry "Havoc!" Howl, "Malice!" for the Abomination
of Desolation prowls the rooms of the house.

Wally: "Where's salvation? Could death and its grieving
melt this stone of ice and release my family?"

But who should lay his neck on the fireman's altar?
Not his siblings, nor his parents. He alone, for he

alone has conceived this blood-sacrifice
to unite his family as they were in Chicago.

The heat of his love might melt the iron bars
of their captivity and set them free.

PART 2

Kinder- und Hausmärchen

Komm! Folge mir. Leibchen, fasse mut!
Come, my dear one. Pluck up your courage and follow me.

From Goethe's *Faust*, Part One

I

My mother's tongue was wooden, straight, a broom
projecting from her mouth, her hair the brambles.
She cleaned house like the north wind, cold, grim—

Grimms! You brothers found her *ungesammelt*
in God knows what *bauern* cottages—
What did it serve, putting her back together?
Philology? Damn reckless sciences!

My mother's tongue was wooden. Write that after
you've written how she licked my skin the way
the medieval bear licked her cubs to shape.

My mother's mouth was wooden. Alice may
have met the duchess peppered, yet she escaped
that grim cottage. But I—my mother's face
was Teuton—I lived the tale as commonplace.

II

Yet we blame our mothers, never thinking that the tale
that tells our childhoods tells her tale too.

But what was a woman permitted? If she were frail
she'd break. *Storm, then, through another summer.*

If she were passionate they'd damn her as a gypsy *(though
passion was proper for raising proper children).*

If poems thrilled her; if she wept at the swoop
of a swallow; if she danced more wildly than she should,

they'd cluck scornfully: "Send her to Bedlam!"
If she laughed too loosely, "She's hysterical!

The woman's uterus is wandering!"
Then let her outface her accusing rabble.

For she is the Dilly Queen in lavender,
the Cinderella Princess wearing purple.

III

I remember your cellar, now. Do you?
Clean concrete tubs, a glass-ribbed scrubbing board,
and that smell! (Grandma had dry armpit, a bald
pubis, leather intestines, a mouth that chewed
blasphemies while Almighty Lord God
issued ten black chunks of commandments
which grandma threw on her coal pile,
stirring a Sinaitic dust)—that smell was the stink
in your cellar. So here's my question. Were you commanded,
as I was, to bite Fells Naphtha soap and chew it
till it foamed in your mouth because you'd told a lie,
and grandma (the woodcutter's wife) hated lies?
     Gretel, Gretel, we've suffered the same mother.
     I am Hänsel, Hänsel. I am your brother.

IV

Yes, there were monsters in our neighborhood:
faculty wives down faculty row. Faultfinders
finding fault. But they couldn't ruin you
nor you them. It was a stand-off, slander for slander.

Monsters. Sweet Acid Gossip soiled the air.
Your name in the breezes smelled like wet hair.
Clothes-pinning your laundry, you swore silently.
Ironing, your heat conceived hostilities

which failed. Those monstrous women were all one
body, a ball of bees, a fist of snakes,
or Lucifer's spirit. To assault them singly, one
by one, would kill no more than cut a mist.

Returning attack and raging at your foes,
you sent me down faculty row, selling greeting cards
to the wives. But your rage at your foes, felt like at me.
Mother, your words on my tongue were a bristle of barbs,

and your ire a knot stick thrust down my throat.
The little apprentice said, *Stick, beat! Stick, beat!*
I said, "Who should I beat?" The stick said, *Your mother.*
But because she'd shaped my soul, I whispered, "Me."

V

Mother Hölle, do you know how much I loved you?
under the well-water and on greensward meadows?

When they asked, I shook down red, ripe apples.
I walked on bluebells to your dreamly cottage,

There I plumped your pillows, making snow,
and pleased was I to be your obedient boy.

Mother Hölle, your love cast spells
sending me up in water-wet, golden clothes.

In the glare light of the day, I hurried home
flushed with obedience and its reward.

There your mirror, Mother, rushed me snatching
at my clothes. *"Unser Junge is weider hie!"*

Never (I breathed submerged, through my eyes, and through
wish in the well) never did I not love you.

VI

And now I search the bloodred rose
whose blossom cups one pearl (a dew
drop, beautiful and trembling) whose
charm is the *Schamir*, to undo

the doors and set the captive free.
I dreamed you were a nightingale,
but *Zickut* was all you could croak for me.
A wire cage kept you and travail.

I dreamed the bloodred rose, its touch
Alone, would spring your cage and hush
your grief and shift your shape, all three.

A bloodred rose blooms encaged.
Bones are its bars—but I will break
my breast to break you, Mother, free.

PART 3

In the Spirit
of Rilke's *Book of Hours*

Das Lied bleibt schön.
The song is beautiful and permanent.

From Rilke's *Das Stundenbuch*

I

This tribulation—all things still undone—
is a tethered, inchoate swan.

Death is the incomprehensible.
Death divides. Death cracks open the ground
whereon we take our daily stand.
Death lowers us, his contemplations,
gently down upon waters that receive us kindly.

Be joyful in their reception.
Be joyful under the flood of floods
where we are endlessly secure and as regal
as a king in flowing ermine and purple robes.

Death, calm and composed,
Death descends and deigns
to draw us thither.

II

I trust in that which has never been spoken.
I long to set my most pious feelings free.
What no one has ever dared to do
is not for me a random thing. It is a choice.

I beg you, *mein Gott,* not to think me insolent
for making my powers urgent.
We, never, never angry;
we, always without hesitation;
we, your children, hold you dear. We love you.

I am a small boat tossed on the tide,
a chip on sea's breakers. And now, lying swollen on the shore,
I herald of your vast glory.
I proclaim your name
as none has ever done before.

If this is pride, then I am proud.
My earnest prayers ascend
to your nostrils like the savory smoke
of the evening sacrifice.

III

The watchman builds his hut in the vineyards. He guards
the grapes against the foxes and repels the midnight thieves.
But my hut, Lord, is the security you have fashioned with your
fingers.
I am the night born of your night.

The crooked apple tree still bears fruit.
Fig trees root in marble-hard meadows,
the fruit of your hands. And told-growth stumps sprout
the green shoots that will produce a hundred sweetmeats.

Their perfume is the exhalation of your blossoms.
You do not, because you need not, ask if I'm awake.
And I do not, because I need not, answer that I'm unafraid,
for you have spread over me the shadow of your mantle.

IV

Shadows hover over my daily labors
like a forest canopy, and I am the loam below.
When I pray, I paint my supplications on the air.

On every Sunday I am Jubilation
in the valley of Jerusalem.

I am pride in the city of God.
I am the song that sings in a hundred voices.
David's thanksgivings fade within me.
I am the harpist whose music
is the melody of the evening star.

My winding passageways arise like a lace.
I have been long abandoned,
and yet I increase.
I can hear the tread
that enlarges loneliness, even from the beginning
of Beginnings.

PART 4

Eight Descents

I know the bottom, she says. I know it with my great tap root.

From Sylvia Plath's "Elm"

1, KEEPSAKE

You, my children—I have no legacy
to leave you except my stories. An old man's lips
tremble. His eyes grow dim, eclipsed by age.
His scalp balds and blotches, and his grinders cease
because they are few. As for my tales, you will quarry
them as men quarry the stones of Carrara.

I can't remain in what you choose to change,
and you *will* choose when I cannot. Stories are
patchworks of fairy tales and the searchings of poets.
Stories are as hoary and as unforgot
and as vulvar as the *Heilgeschichte,* cursing its hearers
and blessing them with one mouth and one tongue.

Vexed by my impoverished legacy,
you'll mine my tales for some a rich vein, crying,
"Dammit! We'll make our *own* inheritance!"

2, MERE OBLIVION

In winter, under a dawn vastly grey,
on a catatonic snow, stands an old man,

his eyebrows rimed, his eye like the crosshairs
of a rifle's scope. He has chambered one cartridge

in his .22. His eye will be unerring.
He'll carry home meat to fill his old wife's pot.

The hunter plans, in the greydawn underneath,
to pierce mid-winter with a single shot.

There. A hare lop-walks on the crusted snow.
He fixes on her, then *cracks!* the midwinter air.

Two eyes are soldered out. A short distemper
shakes the hare's bones. Death stalks the snow.

She grooms her paws with quick, bloody licks,
then lies down on eternity's endlessly white fields.

3, VARIATIONS ON IMMORTALITY

She's a flying thread-knot with pine-sliver limbs,
constructed of bitterness and accident
in the time of the seventh seal, when heaven was shut.

You sing your hymns, Herbert, and I'll sing mine,
and the one who sings encomiums to a mosquito
knows right well the unrighteous Deity.

You drink the sacred blood of your Jesus Christ.
I'll allow the mosquito to drink *my* blood.
You pray, "Thy power and love, my love and trust."

Me? I'll bastardize your own words:
"Things present shrink and die." You praise his Presence,
George, and I will rummage through his Absence.

I'll mourn the little creature's little spleen
until she dawdles through a second birth.

4, REJECTED? REALLY?

Am I like the Christian who's overstayed his welcome
in the Church Universal? Do you accuse me, saying
that my breath breathes corruption in the air of your nave?
Believers hiss, then excommunicate.

They hound the poor pug into outer darkness.
They bullet their hymns. They whip the cur with their creeds.
Luther hated Jews. Rome despised
Luther. Three corbies on wires glared scornfully down.

So, flay my hair. Stuff my mouth with apples.
Bake me. Lay me salted on your platter.
Slice me. Serve me succulent, and I
will be the mutton that feeds your Easter feast.

Lonely walks the black rim of the cosmos.
Fear stays my feet from leaping down.

5, WHAT IS LOST

I regard the sun
as a pan, frying
on the troposphere.
God *damn* its "Gloria!"

I hate, I hate
its hostility
and the sun's rant:
"Anathema!"

The moon subdues
that firework, herself
a discus that can slice
skin—and yet,

I miss that light
gone too soon.

6, THE SANDS OF TIME

When time and times and half a time consume
the world in the fiery, fathomless pit the Hebrews
called *sheol,* and before the serpent uncoils its length,

try hiding in caverns. Stones will break stones.
Under the sea? Consider Behemoth.
In the night? The lunatic moon will madden you.

Heaven's staccato lightning will stipple the world
on a spider's long legs. Continents will quake,
and shooting stars will fracture the firmament.

Get you up to the clouds on high mountains.
Lift your hands. Worship the raging day.
Beseech earth's umbra to shroud the moon.

Time and times and half a time are sands
in the hourglasses of geologists.

7, A METEORIC RIDE

The monk's habit is infested with fleas.
The sarcastic sun blisters his tonsured head.
Labor has knot-gnarled his knuckles. His ascending
prayers are a noxious smoke in the nostrils of God.

Brothers betray brothers to death, and fathers their children,
and children their parents. America lasers Iran.
The president imprisons immigrants.
Lies are the locusts that plague the internet.

Pandemic encircles the globe. Humanity
succumbs. The children of men are being interred
in coffins sawn from Lombardy poplars.
Stars weep blood. Mountains vomit lava.

The poet rides a meteor, writing
poems the ends of which he does not know.

8, THE STOIC

I've drunk three cups of baptismal water, and eaten stones transformed into nuts and berries. And I lift my spirits by drinking a chalice of bloody Mary standing on her celery pedestal.

Hoc est corpus is nothing more than "hocus pocus."

I am the ungodly who makes himself godly, and I will dispute anyone who says otherwise.

There is a valley of shadows wherein I walk—a mortal immortalized.

I have indulged myself in Epicurean pleasures.

I am Zeno: nothing in the world is the Good save virtue. I am Seneca. Virtue is an indifference to death. I am Jean-Paul Sartre. Nothing is.

I offer myself as a philosophical model. Put period to your syntax.

PART 5

Finis

Death, the engraver, puts forward his bone foot.

From Robert Lowell's "At the Indian Killer's Grave"

THE END

Dies irae, dies illa,	That day of wrath, that last day
Solvet saeclum favilla;	will incinerate the world to ashes, ashes,
Teste David cum Sibylla.	as David and Sibyl prophesied.
Quantus tremor est futurus,	When humans are arraigned before
Quando judex est venturus	the judge whose strict inquisition will probe
Cuncta stricta discussurus.	their faults, they will all stagger with fright.
Tuba mirum spargence sonum	The mouths of tombs are the mouths of trumpets
Per sepulchral regionum,	sounding commandments to the four corners:
Coget omnes ante thronum.	"Come ye! Cringe at the foot of the throne!"
Mors stupebit et natura,	Nature, even Death, will be shocked
Cum resurget creatura,	when creation arises and is required
Judicanti responsura.	to defend itself before the Judge.

W. M. Wangerin
Revised, May 7, 2020

Made in the USA
Middletown, DE
11 December 2020